KERI DAVIES

WHO'S WHO IN

The Archers

2001

To Toby, Nathan and Daniel.
They know who they are . . .

This book is published to accompany the BBC Radio 4 serial *The Archers*.
The editor of *The Archers* is Vanessa Whitburn.

Published by BBC Worldwide Ltd, Woodlands,
80 Wood Lane, London W12 0TT

First published 1999
This updated edition published 2000
Copyright © BBC 2000

ISBN: 0 563 53717 5

Commissioning Editor: Emma Shackleton
Project Editor: Anthony Brennan
Design: Lisa Pettibone
Text set in Garamond Light 10.5/14pt
Printed and Bound in Great Britain by Martins of Berwick Ltd
Cover printed by Belmont Press

Events in Ambridge are constantly changing, but we have done our best to make
Who's Who in The Archers 2001 accurate at the time of publication.

¥ WELCOME TO AMBRIDGE ¥

This is the second commercial edition of a book that started life as an in-house publication put together by *The Archers'* production team.

It was intended originally as a helpful guide to new listeners but to our pleasure we have found that even long standing Archers aficionados find plenty to discover and enjoy inside.

So if you're having trouble sorting your Cyril Hoods from your Clive Horrobins (and believe me their initials are the only thing they have in common) or wondered what connects Lilian Bellamy and Wayne Foley*, this book is for you.

Vanessa Whitburn
Editor, *The Archers*

(*Wayne works with Brenda Tucker at Radio Borsetshire. Brenda's brother Roy is the father of Phoebe Aldridge. Phoebe's mother Kate is Lilian's niece. Easy, see?)

In Whit Week 1950, the BBC's Midlands Home Service broadcast five pilot episodes of a new, experimental drama series: *The Archers*. Its creator Godfrey Baseley had previously worked mainly on agricultural programmes. He hoped that farmers would listen for the stories, but along the way pick up messages that would help them feed a Britain still subject to food rationing. Baseley achieved his ambition for the programme. But he also created a broadcasting institution that is still reflecting rural Britain in the 21st century.

The Archers' official birthday was on 1 January 1951, when for the first time the lively 'dum-di-dum' of Arthur Wood's maypole dance *Barwick Green* introduced episode one to a national audience.

Despite half a century of change, the Ambridge of episode 13,169, broadcast on 1 January 2001, would still be recognisable to its post-war inhabitants. Conversation over the farm gate may now be about genetically modified crops or the world trade talks, but March still brings lambing and in August farmers still hope their harvest will be blessed with sunshine.

The Archers lost its original, educational, purpose in the early 1970s, but it still prides itself on the quality of its research and its reflection of real rural life. The Editor, Vanessa Whitburn, leads an eight-strong production team and nine writers as they plot the twists and turns of the families in Ambridge, looking ahead months or sometimes years in biannual long-term meetings. The detailed planning is done at monthly script meetings about two months ahead of trans- mission. Each writer produces a week's worth of scripts in a remarkable 14 days. To retain listeners' attention in the early years, *Archers* writers drew on the tradition of the "cliffhanger" which was so much part of its predecessor, the thriller serial *Dick Barton, Special Agent!* The modern equivalent are stories carefully planned and structured to captivate today's sophisticated audience.

Actors receive their scripts a few days before recording, which takes place every four weeks in Studio 3 at BBC Pebble Mill in Birmingham. Twenty-four episodes are recorded in six intensive days, using only two hours of studio time per thirteen minute episode. This schedule means that being an Archers actor is by no means a full time job, even for major characters, so many also have careers in film, theatre, television or other radio drama.

The episodes are transmitted three to six weeks after recording. But listeners are occasionally intrigued to hear topical events reflected in that evening's broadcast, a feat achieved through a flurry of rewriting, re-recording and editing on the day of transmission.

In the UK, *The Archers* goes out on BBC Radio 4 (FM 92.4–94.6, LW 198). For decades, troops overseas kept in touch with this little piece of home via the British Forces Broadcasting Service, and ex-pats received cassettes recorded by family or friends. But listeners worldwide can now tune into Ambridge without burdening the postal system or taking the Queen's shilling – via the Archers website*.

In the 1950s, the only website people would have recognised was a spider's nest. But *The Archers* has changed as the world has changed, and the four and a half million listeners who follow events in Ambridge still find it as relevant and compelling as those who tuned in half a century ago to that first "dum-di-dum".

Keri Davies
Senior Producer, *The Archers*

*Website: www.bbc.co.uk/radio4/archers
Transmission times are the same as for Radio 4: 19.02 GMT/BST Sunday to Friday, repeated at 14.02 the next day (excluding Saturdays). Omnibus edition of the whole week's episodes every Sunday at 10.00.

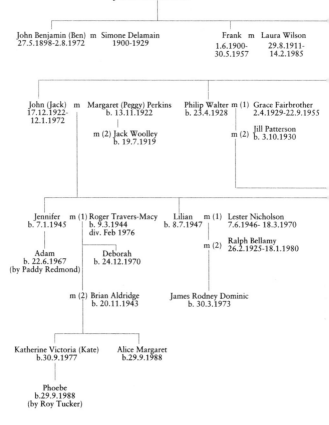

John Archer m Phoebe

John Benjamin (Ben) m Simone Delamain
27.5.1898-2.8.1972   1900-1929

Frank m Laura Wilson
1.6.1900-   29.8.1911-
30.5.1957   14.2.1985

John (Jack) m Margaret (Peggy) Perkins
17.12.1922-   b. 13.11.1922
12.1.1972
              m (2) Jack Woolley
              b. 19.7.1919

Philip Walter m (1) Grace Fairbrother
b. 23.4.1928   2.4.1929-22.9.1955

          m (2) Jill Patterson
                b. 3.10.1930

Jennifer m (1) Roger Travers-Macy
b. 7.1.1945   b. 9.3.1944
                div. Feb 1976

Adam   Deborah
b. 22.6.1967   b. 24.12.1970
(by Paddy Redmond)

Lilian m (1) Lester Nicholson
b. 8.7.1947   7.6.1946- 18.3.1970

        m (2) Ralph Bellamy
              26.2.1925-18.1.1980

m (2) Brian Aldridge
      b. 20.11.1943

James Rodney Dominic
b. 30.3.1973

Katherine Victoria (Kate)   Alice Margaret
b.30.9.1977   b.29.9.1988

Phoebe
b.29.9.1988
(by Roy Tucker)

8

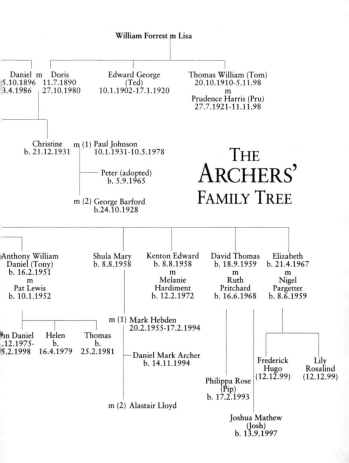

William Forrest m Lisa

Daniel m Doris
5.10.1896 11.7.1890
3.4.1986 27.10.1980

Edward George
(Ted)
10.1.1902-17.1.1920

Thomas William (Tom)
20.10.1910-5.11.98
m
Prudence Harris (Pru)
27.7.1921-11.11.98

Christine m (1) Paul Johnson
b. 21.12.1931   10.1.1931-10.5.1978

Peter (adopted)
b. 5.9.1965

m (2) George Barford
b.24.10.1928

THE ARCHERS' FAMILY TREE

Anthony William
Daniel (Tony)
b. 16.2.1951
m
Pat Lewis
b. 10.1.1952

Shula Mary
b. 8.8.1958

Kenton Edward
b. 8.8.1958
m
Melanie
Hardiment
b. 12.2.1972

David Thomas
b. 18.9.1959
m
Ruth
Pritchard
b. 16.6.1968

Elizabeth
b. 21.4.1967
m
Nigel
Pargetter
b. 8.6.1959

John Daniel
.12.1975-
5.2.1998

Helen
b.
16.4.1979

Thomas
b.
25.2.1981

m (1) Mark Hebden
20.2.1955-17.2.1994

Daniel Mark Archer
b. 14.11.1994

m (2) Alastair Lloyd

Philippa Rose
(Pip)
b. 17.2.1993

Joshua Mathew
(Josh)
b. 13.9.1997

Frederick
Hugo
(12.12.99)

Lily
Rosalind
(12.12.99)

ALICE ALDRIDGE

Home Farm • Born 29.9.88

Twelve going on 26, Alice is **Jennifer** and **Brian**'s second child together. She is a day girl at a local private school and as she's keen on dancing she's regularly pushed into whatever spotlight Jennifer can manoeuvre her way. But Alice's supposed sophistication crumbled at **Ambridge**'s 1999 pantomime when fellow babe in the wood **Christopher Carter** tried to hold her hand. It took **Simon Gerrard**'s cajoling to get her out of the loo and back onstage, but then Simon has a very persuasive way with young females.

BRIAN ALDRIDGE

Home Farm • Born 20.11.43
(Charles Collingwood)

Brian runs **Home Farm** as efficiently as he can, which means big fields, big machines and big subsidy cheques. But big fish Brian found himself swimming with sharks when he became a partner in **Borchester Land** (and landlord to brother-in-law **Tony Archer**). Come the revolution, he'd be one of the first swinging from a lamppost, but shafts of humanity glint occasionally through Brian's well-tailored facade. He opposed the eviction of the **Grundys**, and he's been on tenterhooks since stepdaughter **Debbie**'s marriage to **Simon Gerrard**, whom he's sure is a philanderer. Brian should know. He's had a roving eye in the past, which settled on the fragrant and willing **Caroline Pemberton**, and the comely but unwilling **Betty Tucker**. **Jennifer** has her suspicions about the horsey **Mandy Beesborough**, too …

🐄 JENNIFER ALDRIDGE 🐄

(formerly Travers-Macy, née Archer)
Home Farm • Born 7.1.45
(*Angela Piper*)

Jennifer, the elder daughter of **Peggy Woolley** and her late husband Jack Archer, caused quite a stir in 1967 when she became an unmarried mother with her first son **Adam** (now **Macy**). She later married Roger Travers-Macy who adopted Adam, and they had one daughter, **Debbie** (now **Gerrard**). The marriage did not last, and Jennifer wed **Brian** in 1976. But when Roger returned to **Ambridge** fifteen years later, the embers of passion flared brightly again, albeit briefly. While Brian insists Jennifer is nothing but a compulsive shopper, she has been a teacher, journalist and published author. But nowadays much of her energies and intelligence are taken up with worrying about her wayward daughter **Kate**, and trying to keep the peace between Brian and Debbie.

KATE ALDRIDGE

'Look, I'm a citizen of the world, OK?'
Born 30.9.77
(Kellie Bright)

Eco-warrior Kate, **Jennifer** and **Brian**'s first daughter together, has always kicked against the claustrophobic constraints of **Ambridge**, often disappearing with traveller friends for months on end. Having scandalised the village with her open consumption of drugs, she seemed to take a step forward when she toured the festivals with a vegetarian food business in partnership with then boyfriend **Roy Tucker**. But soon after a bitter break-up, Kate found she was pregnant and fought hard against Roy's attempts to prove himself **Phoebe**'s father. But the pressures of bringing up a child when she still had a lot of growing up to do herself became too much for Kate, and she fled to 'find herself' in Africa. Roy found himself a full time father as a result.

PHOEBE ALDRIDGE

Nightingale • Born 28.6.98

Product of the rather incongruous relationship between clean cut **Roy Tucker** and dreadlocked, noseringed **Kate Aldridge**, this little mite was born in a teepee at the Glastonbury Festival, was prevented from leaving the country by a court order, has been subjected to DNA testing and was named in a new age ceremony on Lakey Hill. Since Roy took her on following Kate's departure to Africa, Phoebe's life has been rather less dramatic, and Roy's girlfriend **Hayley Jordan** loves Phoebe as if she was her own. But if Kate ever returns from her travels she isn't likely to view that arrangement with much delight.

'**S**ituated 6 miles from the market town of **Borchester** and within easy commuting distance of Birmingham, this picturesque and highly desirable village offers good local amenities (shop, pub, children's playground etc) in a charming countryside setting. Local attractions include historic church, village green with duck pond, walks on Lakey Hill and nearby Heydon Berrow. Sporting activities include golf, health club and swimming pool, riding, village cricket team, shooting (game and clays), fishing on the River Am etc. Other activities include active Women's Institute branch, Over 60's club, amateur dramatics. Twinned with **Meyruelle** (France). **Hollerton Junction** station 6 miles.'

– extract from house particulars, Messrs Rodway and Watson, Estate Agents, Borchester.

An uninspired six bedroomed Victorian edifice improved by its mellowing yellow brick and wooden shutters, Ambridge Hall is home to **Lynda** and **Robert Snell**. The landscaped gardens sweeping down to the River Am reflect one of Lynda's passions – garden design and have recently been adapted according to the principles of Feng Shui, much to Robert's irritation. The low allergen area reflects Lynda's Achilles' heel – hay fever.

🐕 MARJORIE ANTROBUS 🐕

Nightingale Farm • Born 1922
(Margot Boyd)

Sprightly widow Marjorie – "Mrs A", as she's known to many villagers – travelled the world helping her husband Teddy prop up the fading British Empire. She was once a renowned breeder of Afghan hounds, but now contents herself with just one Afghan – Bettina – and a cocker spaniel, Charlie, whom she took on when **Nelson Gabriel** disappeared. Bastion of the Parish Council and the PCC, she always provides staunch support to **Ambridge**'s vicars and occasionally deputises for **Phil Archer** as church organist or panto accompanist. Marjorie is a great hostess and occasionally takes in paying guests. The most recent to experience the thickening waistband brought on by the Antrobus layer cake was the equally kindly **Hayley Jordan**, who helped Marjorie recover her confidence at the wheel after a cataract operation.

DAVID ARCHER

Brookfield Bungalow • Born 18.9.59
(Timothy Bentinck)

Although David is not the eldest son, he was the only one of the children interested in farming, and he and wife **Ruth** have progressively taken over more of the running of **Brookfield**. But when **Phil** decided it was time to retire properly, younger daughter **Elizabeth** (**Pargetter**) objected to his plans to pass the farm on wholesale to them. David valiantly overcame the desire to clip his little sister round the ear and tried to find a compromise. But their plans were blown out of the water when Ruth discovered she had breast cancer. David worked as never before to keep the farm running while supporting Ruth through her ordeal. The combination of hard times in farming, Phil's impending retirement and Ruth's illness mean that David faces an uncertain future.

Bridge Farm • Born 16.4.79

Helen breezed through her GCSEs and went on to an HND in food technology at Reaseheath Agricultural College. She now runs **Bridge Farm**'s organic shop in **Borchester** (Ambridge Organics) in a similarly breezy way. Away studying and working for many months after her brother John's death, she returned to find that his ex-girlfriend **Hayley Jordan** had become almost part of the family. There was a messy falling out. Organic sausages and yoghurt pot labels became metaphorical weapons, as Helen struggled to regain her influence on the family and eject the cuckoo from the nest. Helen got her way; Hayley is no longer involved in any Bridge Farm business activities, although **Pat** still has a soft spot for her. So does Helen – at the bottom of **Tony**'s silage clamp.

(née Patterson)

Born 3.10.30 • Brookfield Farm

(Patricia Greene)

To the casual observer, Jill might appear to be the archetypal farmer's wife, helping with the lambing and haymaking, serving on the parish council and delivering meals-on-wheels, while with her other hand bringing up four children – **Kenton, Shula** (now **Hebden Lloyd**), **David** and **Elizabeth** (now **Pargetter**). But this staunch WI member and ex-churchwarden has a radical streak, and will often stand up to **Phil** when she feels strongly on a point of principle. Her adult children – and many villagers – have always been able to turn to Jill for help and advice. But lately she has been in need of a sympathetic ear herself. Seeing her family rent by the quarrel over the inheritance of **Brookfield** was terrible enough, but daughter-in-law **Ruth**'s cancer was in a different league altogether.

JOSH ARCHER

Brookfield Bungalow • Born 13.9.97

When **Ruth** went into labour, keen cricketer **David** was in the middle of the innings of a lifetime, but he was persuaded to leave the field to see his son born. **Jill** has often looked after Josh when his parents were busy on the farm, and with Ruth's illness, Josh has continued to see a lot of his grandmother.

KENTON ARCHER

Sydney area
Born 8.8.58
(Graeme Kirk)

Elder son of **Phil** and **Jill**, and **Shula**'s twin, Kenton has caused his parents a lot of worry over the years. His business ambitions have never matched his talents, although his latest scheme – running sailing trips in Australia – seemed to be going well. But when he returned unannounced in 1997, it was some time before he was forced to confess that not only were the Australian authorities pursuing him for a tax debt, but that a marriage of convenience to young, attractive **Mel** had turned into a love match. Phil had to bail him out yet again, and as Kenton had already had his share of the **Brookfield** inheritance when he fancied going into the antique business, this handout was counted a belated wedding present.

MEL ARCHER

(neé Hardiment)
Sydney area • Born 12.2.72

Australian wife of **Kenton Archer**. The family was pleased for Mel and **Kenton** when they heard she was pregnant in August 2000. But given that **Ruth** was undergoing chemotherapy which could make her infertile, the timing could have been better.

🌳 PAT ARCHER 🌳

(née Lewis)
Bridge Farm • Born 10.1.52
(Patricia Gallimore)

Young, Welsh and determined, Pat swept **Tony** off his feet in 1974 and has made sweeping changes to his life ever since. One of Tony's shrewdest moves was to suggest converting **Bridge Farm** to organic production, a common cause which has been one of the buttresses of the marriage. As Bridge Farm yoghurt and ice cream grew in popularity, Pat progressed from '80s radical to '90s entrepreneur, but she does her best to cling to her principles and be a good employer. The first anniversary of the death of their son John threw Pat into months of clinical depression, but Tony knew she was back to her old self when she came up with ambitious plans to open an organic farm shop in **Borchester**, now run by daughter **Helen**.

PHIL ARCHER

Brookfield Farm • Born 23.4.28
(Norman Painting)

Son of the late Dan and Doris Archer. When Phil lost his first wife Grace in a stable fire in 1955, he was too grief-stricken to note that it coincided with the launch of something called ITV. Although devastated at the time, Phil eventually became captivated by a travelling sales demonstrator **Jill** Patterson, and they were married in 1957. After a lifetime farming, Phil planned to ease himself into retirement and spend more time on his off-duty activities; he is the organist at the parish church of **St Stephen's** and his piano playing often accompanies village productions. But the need to take money out of the farm to buy a retirement house, and daughter **Elizabeth Pargetter**'s objections to the whole deal, turned the Archers into a family at war with itself.

PIP ARCHER

Brookfield Bungalow • Born 17.2.93
(Helen Palmer)

Philippa Rose, or "Pip" as parents **Ruth** and **David** call her, came into the world at 4.16pm on 17th February 1993 weighing 8 pounds and half an ounce. Pip took well to Loxley Barratt Primary School until brother **Josh** came along, when she started to play up. David eventually solved the jealousy by allowing Pip to show off her brother to her classmates. She was old enough to realise that her mother was very ill, and David had to do a lot of reassuring that Ruth was getting better, despite appearances.

RUTH ARCHER

(née Pritchard)

Brookfield Bungalow • Born 16.6.68

(Felicity Finch)

Ruth came from Prudoe in Northumberland to work at **Brookfield** as an agricultural student, and married **David** in 1988. Slowly, with ideas such as establishing a co-op to save money on cattle feed, she gained the respect of local farmers. She continued to farm after **Pip** and **Josh** were born, with special responsibility for the dairy herd, and spearheaded many innovations at Brookfield. Ruth and David were facing the challenge of taking on the farm on their own when Ruth was stricken with breast cancer, and she needed all her fight to cope with a mastectomy and punishing chemotherapy. Even if she survives, Ruth will face tormenting uncertainty. Will David still find her attractive? Will she be able to have another baby? And, of course, will the cancer recur?

🐖 THOMAS (TOMMY) ARCHER 🐖

Bridge Farm • Born 25.2.81
(Tom Graham)

Tommy (he'd prefer you to call him Tom) had a real struggle after his brother John's death, which with awful timing happened on Tommy's 17th birthday. Tommy's desire to fill his dead brother's boots led him to ditch his A Level studies for a day release course at Borsetshire Agricultural College. **Pat** was dismayed at the time, but it's worked out pretty well. Tommy helps his father on the farm and runs the outdoor herd of Gloucester Old Spot pigs which John established. Pat and **Tony** understood Tommy's motives when in 1999 he and some friends attacked a trial crop of genetically modified oil seed rape at **Home Farm**, but when he faced a possible prison sentence for criminal damage they went through agonies until his acquittal.

Bridge Farm • Born 16.2.51
(Colin Skipp)

Jennifer Aldridge's brother and only son of **Peggy Woolley** and her late husband Jack Archer. Tony's daily grind provides the veg for the farm shop, and the milk which his more entrepreneurial wife **Pat** processes in the dairy. You'd seldom describe Tony as 'cheerful', especially when he is lifting leeks, but he's a hard worker, a good stockman and strongly committed to the organic cause – and there's always a pint or three in **The Bull** to ease the stresses of the day. For a long time, Tony felt responsible for the loss of his elder son John in a tractor accident in 1998. Each anniversary of the death is slightly easier to bear, but he could do without the need for continual peacekeeping operations between his remaining offspring **Tommy** and **Helen**.

JEAN-PAUL AUBERT

Grey Gables • Born 1951
(Yves Aubert)

Head chef at Grey Gables and one of the reasons for its continuing success, Jean Paul's great strength is that he will never compromise. Unfortunately, that is also his great weakness. It is lucky that no-one is better able to defuse a Jean-Paul tantrum than his friend and manager **Caroline Pemberton**. If the bottom ever drops out of the hotel business, Caroline would seem ideally qualified for a job in, say, bomb disposal.

Vaguely New Age and definitely undesirable, Baggy is one of the bad influences on **Eddie Grundy** (as if Eddie *needed* any bad influences, **Clarrie** would say). Baggy is a garage mechanic by trade and a drinker by inclination, with a wide selection of dodgy acquaintances. He has numerous children with his girlfriend Sylvia, amongst them Aslan, China, Sunshine and Buttercup.

BANNISTERS

Trendy café bar where the bright things of Borsetshire go to sparkle. The owner started with just one outlet, but soon controlled five, each with its own character and clientèle. He later moved into the food production business, supplying ready-made items to his previous outlets, and subsequently into marketing and publicity.

CHRISTINE BARFORD

(Formerly Johnson, née Archer)
The Stables • Born 21.12.31
(Lesley Saweard)

Phil Archer's sister owns a riding school and livery business. Since back trouble ended Christine's days in the saddle, her partner and niece **Shula Hebden Lloyd** does most of the teaching while Chris handles the office work. Practical and resilient, Chris (as she's known in the family) worked hard with horses all her life, while for many years struggling with marriage to an airy dreamer, Paul Johnson. After his death, Christine found happiness with the altogether more down-to-earth **George**. Peter, her adopted son from her first marriage, lives away from the village. Chris spent several years persuading George to retire, and then he spent several months persuading her to do the same. At last, they're enjoying having more time together.

GEORGE BARFORD

The Stables • Born 24.10.28
(Graham Roberts)

A former policeman, George worked for twenty-five years as the gamekeeper at **Grey Gables** and now busies himself with voluntary work as a tree warden. Like his current wife, **Christine**, George is on his second marriage, and he has two children, Karen and Terry, from the first one. He had hoped that Terry might follow in his gamekeeping footsteps, but he had better success in bringing on young **William Grundy**. A straight talking Yorkshireman, George is a reformed alcoholic, so you'll seldom see him in **The Bull**, and then only with an orange juice. He plays the cornet and makes a popular chairman of the Parish Council.

🐎 MANDY BEESBOROUGH 🐎

Loxley Barratt • Born 1953

Now what on earth would **Brian Aldridge** see in a vivacious, red-headed jodhpur-clad Pony Club instructor? 'Absolutely nothing, darling', as Brian told **Jennifer**. So that's all right then...

BERROW ESTATE

See BORCHESTER LAND

LILIAN BELLAMY

(formerly Nicholson, née Archer)
Guernsey • Born 8.7.47
(Elizabeth Marlowe)

Jennifer Aldridge's younger sister. Lilian's second husband Ralph Bellamy was probably the last real squire figure in **Ambridge**, and **Shula Hebden Lloyd** acquired much of her equestrian skills under Lilian's tutelage. In the 1970s, Ralph's heart condition forced him to opt for a quieter life in the warmth of Guernsey and so Lilian withdrew from her previously prominent position in the village. Since Ralph's death in 1980, Lilian seems to have found comfort mainly in gin, and in the company of well-built young men. What her son James – born in 1973 and now living in London – thinks about this is not on record. Of course, having two wealthy sisters has made **Tony Archer** very well balanced – he has a chip on both shoulders.

'**A** busy market town displaying pleasant if unexceptional vernacular architecture and sadly little evidence of its Roman origins. Accommodation includes The Feathers Hotel (comfortable), and a variety of eating establishments (Botticelli – good but pricey, Star of Bombay – basic balti). Not a shopper's paradise, but some interest to be found at **Underwoods** department store and smaller specialist shops (good sausages to be had at Ambridge Organics, Harcourt Road). Municipal leisure centre/gym and swimming pool for the active visitor. Theatre Royal and small multiplex cinema for the more indolent. Also a suitable base for exploring the pleasant villages of the Am Vale – once you have negotiated the often congested by-pass.'

From *Travels through the English Shires, Volume 2 – The Midlands*, by Seymour A. Roads

Property company owning the 1020 acre Berrow Estate. The sale of **Grange Farm** means that **Bridge Farm** is now the Estate's only tenanted holding. **Brian Aldridge** is a small shareholder and farms the "in-hand" land on contract to the company. **Matt Crawford** is a rather bigger one (shareholder, that is), and was without doubt the prime mover in the eviction of the **Grundys**. This, like all the company's actions are dictated by the inexorable logic of maximising return on capital. They failed to get planning permission for a small housing development, and have discussed a leisure complex, but not taken plans forward. So far, the face of **Ambridge** has not been radically altered, but Borchester Land will keep trying.

BRIDGE FARM

STOCK
65 milkers (Friesian) • 30 followers (heifers/calves)
100 outdoor reared pigs

CROPS
115 acres grassland • 22 acres barley
15 acres wheat • 6 acres potatoes • 2 acres carrots
2 acres leeks • 3 acres swedes • 2 acres Dutch
cabbage • 1 acre Savoy cabbage • 4 acres mixed
vegetable and salad crops

LABOUR
Tony Archer • **Pat Archer** • **Tommy Archer**
Clarrie Grundy, Colin Kennedy (dairy)
Contract labour during harvest/silage/etc
Occasional students

Tenant farmers **Tony** and **Pat Archer** rent 140 acres from the **Berrow Estate**, with an extra 32 acres from other landlords. Bridge Farm converted to organic in 1984. The dairy's yoghurt and ice cream is sold through a wholesaler and to local outlets such as the **Village Shop**, **Grey Gables** and **Underwoods**. But Pat and Tony would first direct you to their own farm shop Ambridge Organics in **Borchester**, which also stocks their own sausages and other meat from the herd of Gloucester Old Spots.

BROOKFIELD FARM

STOCK
110 milkers (Friesian) • 70 followers (heifers/calves)
20 beef cattle (all ages) • 300 ewes
hens (small scale)

CROPS
258 acres grassland • 115 acres cereals
34 acres oil seed rape • 15 acres potatoes
12 acres beans • 10 acres fodder beet
17 acres forage maize • 8 acres set-aside

LABOUR

Phil Archer (managing and relief)
David Archer (partner, mainly arable)
Ruth Archer (partner, mainly dairy)
Jill Archer (partner, hens, bees)
Bert Fry (general)
Jet (sheepdog)

Brookfield is a 469 acre mixed farm, which also carries out contracting work for **Home Farm** and the **Berrow Estate**. In 2000, **Phil** and **Jill Archer** decided to retire from the running of the farm and give **David** and daughter-in-law **Ruth** full control (and allow them to move into Brookfield's comfortable farmhouse). But plans were stalled because of family objections and the discovery of Ruth's cancer. Whatever the future for Brookfield, it will almost certainly have to streamline its activities, probably concentrating on dairy and arable.

THE BULL

'*While in **Ambridge**, be sure to visit The Bull, a real old English pub in the care of **Sid ~~and Kathy~~ Perks**. This quaint half-timbered building is in a charming setting just off the Village Green and features a taste of France, with its own boules pitch or piste, home to the Ambridge Bulls team. Enjoy a game of darts or dominoes in the traditional bar, or relax in the cosy Ploughman's Bar. Extensive bar snack menu. Or for a full meal, there's our Family Restaurant, with satisfying treats at affordable prices (menu may be restricted). Upstairs function room. Beer garden with Eccles the peacock. Free house serving excellent Shires Bitter. No juke box. Coach parties welcome by arrangement. Try our line dancing with Jolene.*'

(A Guide to *Ambridge* leaflet (amended by hand) available at **St Stephen's** church)

🐓 CHRISTOPHER CARTER 🐓

No 1, The Green • Born 22.6.88

Neil and **Susan**'s son, and younger brother to **Emma**, Christopher started at Borchester Green secondary school in September 1999.

EMMA CARTER

No 1, The Green • Born 7.8.84

Neil and **Susan**'s daughter has turned into a sassy teenager and keen dancer. After unspectacular GCSE results, she decided school wasn't for her and to Susan's distress got a job as a kitchen assistant at **Lower Loxley**'s café. (Damn those Horrobin genes.) Emma occasionally deigns to spend time with **Ed Grundy**, which gives you an idea of how short **Ambridge** is of eligible young men.

NEIL CARTER

No 1, The Green • Born 25.5.57
(Brian Hewlett)

Neil used to be **Brookfield**'s pig man, until **Susan** persuaded him to take a job as a feed rep for Borchester Mills. Susan was convinced that Neil's prospects would improve and help pay the mortgage on their "right to buy" council house. But in 1998 unhappy Neil hung up his mobile phone to return to the land. He picks up what employment he can on local farms, and runs a small outdoor breeding herd of Gloucester Old Spot pigs on a few acres which he owns at **Willow Farm**. In 2000, **Ruth** and **David Archer** asked him to run an expanded pig enterprise at Brookfield, but they let him down badly when they realised their plans were unviable. Usually the hired hand, Neil takes control at **St Stephen's** church where he is tower captain of the bellringers.

SUSAN CARTER

(née Horrobin)
No 1, The Green • Born 10.10.63
(Charlotte Martin)

Susan is not a happy woman. She tried hard to rid herself of the shame of originally being a **Horrobin**, but all her upwardly mobile efforts came to nothing when her brother **Clive** robbed the village post office in 1993. She succumbed to family feeling and sheltered him while he was on the run. But Clive proved there's no honour among thieves when he shopped her for her sisterly care, and she spent three months inside as a result. She was devastated when **Neil** resigned his salesman's job and sees herself as the main breadwinner, working part time at the surgery and in the **Village Shop**. She thinks Neil is too nice for his own good, which is probably true, but she does her best to redress the balance.

MATT CRAWFORD

*Somewhere posh near Borchester and a nice
place in town*
(Kim Durham)

East-End-wide-boy-made-good Matt is one of
Brian Aldridge's co-directors in **Borchester
Land**. He thinks Brian is too swayed by local
opinion on controversial development proposals,
and that he panders too much to the straw-
chewing, cider-drinking yokels. Like a stopped
clock, Matt's hands are seldom in the right place,
and **Debbie Aldridge** once had to fight off his
amorous advances (Matt is married, but his wife
stays mainly in London). Brian was able to use
the threat of a sexual harassment charge to
silence Matt around the boardroom table, but it
was just one battle, and Matt definitely got his
own back when the **Grundys** were evicted
without Brian's approval.

ERIC

Willow Farm

Visitors to **Ambridge** may be puzzled to hear talk in the pub of the Danish physicist Niels Bohr. In fact the conversation is probably about Eric, the 100 per cent all male, Playgirl pin-up of the Gloucester Old Spot race. **Tommy Archer** bought him with a loan from his grandmother **Peggy**, but he's on long term loan to **Neil Carter** so that he can supply organic weaners for **Bridge Farm** to fatten to pork weight. 'Neil's boar' likes to wander, and occasionally causes havoc for gardeners when he manages to get through his electric fence.

Cathedral city 17 miles east of **Ambridge**. Despite the attractions of **Underwoods**, Felpersham is where Ambridge residents go when they need an intensive course of retail therapy, followed by a skinny latte at **Bannisters**.

JANET FISHER

The Vicarage, Darrington
(Moir Leslie)

As if Janet didn't have enough to do as vicar of the parishes of Darrington, Penny Hassett and Edgeley, in 1996 the diocese decided she could take over **Ambridge** too. Some parishioners left, rather than countenance a woman priest. But she slowly won round a few doubters and has proved approachable and popular (although not with **Peggy Woolley**, who changed her allegiance to All Saints, **Borchester**). In 1999 Janet left the parish for three weeks to walk from Birmingham to Cologne as part of the campaign to write off Third World debt, a radical gesture which set critical tongues wagging for a while. Janet's erratic punctuality is not helped by her supreme and not always well-founded confidence that she's a dab hand at maintaining her old Triumph Herald.

Glebelands

With his wife Pat, one of the earliest residents of Glebelands, a small development of 'executive homes' near the Green. The Fletchers are the kind of people who move to the country for the air, the views and the wildlife and then complain about the smell, the silage clamps and being woken up by cockerels. Along with **Peggy Woolley**, Derek was one of the parishioners who left **St Stephen's** for All Saints, **Borchester** on the appointment of **Janet Fisher**.

WAYNE FOLEY

🌳   🌳

(Ian Brooker)
BBC Radio Borsetshire
Broadcasting throughout the county on 87.3FM

'*Tune into the Wayne Foley Afternoon Show – with news and views from around the county, the Tea-Time Guest, and Wayne's unique spot the ball contest!*

Something to say? Call Brenda* on the phones.

Every weekday, 2 'til 5.

Take your afternoon tea – tune to Foley.'

(*That's **Brenda Tucker**. **Mike**'s so proud)

Along with **Baggy**, Snatch is one of **Eddie Grundy**'s less desirable friends, who's been seeking asylum in various Borsetshire pubs since the closure of the Cat and Fiddle. He wanted to name his son after Britain's most celebrated boxer and panto star, so the hapless child was christened not Frank, but Bruno.

BERT FRY

Woodbine Cottage • Born 1936
(Eric Allen)

David **Archer** sometimes thinks that his general worker at **Brookfield** has a head as thick as the fodder beet they grow. But Bert's stolid exterior belies the coals of creativity burning within. Often prone to breaking into verse, Bert achieved fame (at least in Borsetshire) with his own column in the *Borchester Echo* and appearances on local television. When he and **Freda** became grandparents in the autumn of 1996, they took an extended holiday to dote on the infant. At least it was wintertime, so it didn't interfere with Bert's duties as cricket umpire, although he was missed from his responsibilities as churchwarden. After a hard day tilling the soil at Brookfield, Bert relishes the total contrast of … tilling the soil in his garden. Don't bother entering the annual Flower and Produce competition, not if you expect to win anything.

Woodbine Cottage.

Many of **The Bull** restaurant's burgers and nuggets are prepared with the help of Freda Fry (was ever a woman so aptly named?), but in her own kitchen she tends to more traditional catering. When husband **Bert** is showing off his unfeasibly large courgettes at the annual Flower and Produce Show, Freda's cakes and chutneys will be sending the judges into ecstasy on a trestle table not far away. She cleans the house and holiday cottage for **Jill Archer** at **Brookfield** as well as keeping her own domain spotless. No surprise then, that she never has time to speak.

NELSON GABRIEL

Your guess is as good as ours
Born 1933
(Jack May, deceased)

With the sale of Honeysuckle Cottage to **Tim** and **Siobhan Hathaway**, the only thing of Nelson's remaining in **Ambridge** is his old bitch Charlie (no, she's a dog... no a real dog, a cocker spaniel. Please...) now in the care of **Marjorie Antrobus**. Once his wine bar was *the* place for a romantic tête à tête, and his antique shop the natural choice for the gift buyer with plenty of money and a trusting nature. But some mysterious financial disaster befell him and he fled the country, leaving behind puzzled friends and a repossession order. They imagine him to be running a bar in Havana or Vientiane, dispensing world-weary drolleries along with the Triple Sec. We shall probably never know.

LUCY GEMMELL

(née Perks)

New Zealand • Born 12.12.71

(Tracey-Jane White)

Lucy was never an easy child, but once her father **Sid Perks** remarried, life became one long war of attrition at **The Bull**. Then, after failing her Environmental Science degree, Lucy married Duncan Gemmell, the son of a Kiwi sheep farmer. Lucy probably wasn't surprised by the eventual break up of her father's marriage to **Kathy**. But what she'll think of **Jolene Rogers** is anyone's guess.

DEBBIE GERRARD

(neé Aldridge)
Woolmarket Flats, Borchester
Born 24.12.70
(Tamsin Greig)

Debbie is the daughter of **Jennifer Aldridge** and her first husband **Roger Travers-Macy**. Having dropped out of university after an affair with her lecturer **Simon Gerrard**, she eventually made a success as **Brian**'s deputy at **Home Farm**. For a while she was less successful with men, but in 1999 Simon returned, professing undiminished love for her. Despite stepfather Brian's certainty that Gerrard is either after her money or will be unfaithful to her or both, Simon and Debbie were married in May 2000. Things have been tricky on the farm ever since. But there is one male who even Brian is happy to see in Debbie's life – her horse Autolycus ("Tolly").

🐕 SIMON GERRARD 🐕

Woolmarket Flats, Borchester
"Hey, you're as old as the woman you feel"
(Garrick Hagon)

Brian Aldridge has nothing but contempt for Simon. Well, all right, he has deep suspicion and loathing too. It looked like Brian's low opinion was justified when a student at the University of Felpersham accused lecturer Simon of sexual harassment. But when the girl withdrew her accusations and herself from the university, **Debbie** accepted Simon's protestations of innocence and a proposal of marriage. Some find Simon's Canadian charm a little too ingratiating and there's no doubt he likes to be liked. But **Jennifer** could chat to him about books for hours.

LADY
MERCEDES GOODMAN

Spanish wife of the wealthy **Sir Sidney Goodman**, and friend to **Julia Pargetter**. Clad in Gucci and Moschino, her appearance can best be described as 'sun-dried'.

🐖 SIR SIDNEY GOODMAN 🐖

This old fascist (he fought with Franco in the Spanish Civil War) still takes a totalitarian approach to running his food processing empire, which includes canning factories in **Borchester**, Spain and elsewhere. Sir Sidney's Spanish interests also extend to his wife **Mercedes**. **Jack Woolley** rather looks up to Sidney Goodman. Jack thinks he could have been as successful, if only he hadn't been quite so soft-hearted.

A working farm (just) until the bankrupt **Grundys** were evicted in April 2000. The bulk of the acreage was absorbed back into the **Berrow Estate** and the farmhouse put up for sale with five acres.

GREY GABLES

*'Facilities ***** Comfort **** Welcome *** Food ***** Value *****

'**S**weeping down the gravel drive, first impressions of this Victorian mock-Gothic mansion overlooking 15 acres of lawn and parkland are very promising. Check-in was handled in a disturbingly efficient manner by a **Mrs Snell**, and a **Mr Higgs** took us in silence to our charming room. In the elegant restaurant, chef **Jean-Paul Aubert** delivers excellent food in the classic French style, although our enjoyment of a delightfully retro Coquilles St Jacques was marred by a noisy altercation in the kitchen, requiring the attention of the composed and efficient manager **Mrs Pemberton**. The proprietor **Mr Woolley** recommended, at length, the Health Club (gym, pool, sauna, etc), 18-hole golf course, conference facilities and...'*

Extract from *Best Hotels in Borsetshire*, Felpersham Press. £7.95 paperback

ALF GRUNDY

Helping Police with their Enquiries
Born 13.11.44

If brother **Eddie** is a loveable rogue and sister-in-law **Clarrie** is loveable, Alf is simply a rogue. He graduated from poaching to receiving stolen goods to breaking and entering, and when released from chokey committed the ultimate sin and stole from his family. While **Joe** retains a shred of paternal feeling for his first-born, Clarrie is in no hurry to see him again.

CLARRIE GRUNDY

A caravan at Willow Farm • Born 12.5.54
(Rosalind Adams)

Long suffering Clarrie is the daughter of the late Jethro Larkin, who used to be a general worker at **Brookfield**. She works part time in **The Bull** and at **Bridge Farm** dairy, and full time to keep her menfolk under control. She once entertained a dream of moving to France, but husband **Eddie** could never be that far from a regular supply of Shires bitter, so she contented herself with helping to twin the village with **Meyruelle**. She has managed to scrape together the cash for occasional trips to France, but the closest the Grundys usually get to a holiday is visiting Clarrie's sister Rosie Mabbett in Great Yarmouth. Clarrie was driven to despair as the family fell apart following their eviction from **Grange Farm**, although Eddie's solution hardly made things easier for her.

EDDIE GRUNDY

A caravan at Willow Farm • Born 15.3.51
(Trevor Harrison)

Younger son of **Joe Grundy** and husband to **Clarrie**. When farm incomes were healthy, Eddie just about managed to keep **Grange Farm** viable, despite wasting his time on dodgy get-rich-quick schemes and attempts to make it as a country and western singer. But the new millennium brought bankruptcy, eviction, and a period of hell in the misleadingly named Meadow Rise flats in **Borchester**. Seeing the dreadful effects this alien environment had on **Joe**, Eddie made an emotional promise that his father would return to **Ambridge**. And so they did, even it if meant a caravan sited illegally on the **Berrow Estate**, property of their erstwhile landlords **Borchester Land**. Son **William** (a gamekeeper on the estate) was much happier when they were offered some more legitimate hard standing by **Neil Carter**.

🐂 EDWARD (ED) GRUNDY 🐂

A caravan at Willow Farm • Born 28.9.84
(Barry Farrimond)

With his can of lager and No 1 haircut, Ed Grundy presents an alarming sight on a dark night, and an even more alarming one during the day. Unlike brother **William**, who knuckled down to his school work at the last minute thanks to his interest in gamekeeping, Ed has no such motivation and is more likely to leave school with a tattoo than a GCSE. **Clarrie** wouldn't have been ecstatic if Ed had shown signs of taking after **Eddie**, but this is much worse. Could he be taking after **Alf**?

JOE GRUNDY

A caravan at Willow Farm • Born 18.9.21
(Edward Kelsey)

A farmer without a farm, Joe was the most affected by the family's enforced transplantation to **Borchester**. He eventually went walkabout in a confused state and nearly died, although you can imagine him preferring death in a ditch in **Ambridge** to life in a fifth floor flat overlooking the canning factory. Once out of hospital, he was supremely happy to be back on his native turf, even if the accommodation rocks in high winds. Joe still misses his wife Susan, dead these thirty years, but a pint of cider always helps to fill the void (although theoretically a Methodist, Joe has never held with that religion's views on Temperance). He suffers from a complaint known as 'farmers lung', which is less useful to him now that there is no work to avoid.

WILLIAM GRUNDY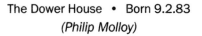

The Dower House • Born 9.2.83
(Philip Molloy)

Eddie taught William all he knew, and then wished he hadn't, as this son of a poacher man chose to pursue a career in gamekeeping. He works as an under-keeper with **Greg Turner** at the combined **Grey Gables** and **Berrow Estate** shoot. When the rest of his family decamped to the horrors of Meadow Rise flats in **Borchester**, William didn't join them. His godmother **Caroline Pemberton** offered him some rooms at the Dower House. With luck like that, he'll be winning the lottery any day now...

SHIV GUPTA

Coventry
(Shiv Grewal)

Accountant Shiv is **Usha Gupta**'s elder brother, and can usually be relied upon to appear at Blossom Hill Cottage when Usha needs cheering up. He didn't really approve of her partner Richard Locke, until they discovered a common passion for cricket. But Shiv was proved right in the end, and when Richard left after that unpleasant business with **Shula Hebden Lloyd**, he did his best not to say 'I told you so'.

USHA GUPTA

Blossom Hill Cottage • Born 1962
(Souad Faress)

Usha's keen sense of fun is sometimes over-whelmed by the demands of her job as a partner in **Felpersham**-based solicitors Jefferson Crabtree. Probably her greatest professional triumph was seeing her client **Tommy Archer** walk free from his GM crop trial. Her parents were unhappy when Usha moved to the country-side from Wolverhampton, especially when she was the target of a gang of racists, in which **Roy Tucker** was initially involved. It was hard to forgive him for that, but even harder to forgive **Shula Hebden Lloyd** for her part in driving away Usha's lover Richard Locke in 1998. The affair remained a source of friction between Shula and Usha's friend **Ruth Archer**, whom Usha has introduced to the sinuous rhythms of her particular passion – salsa dancing.

🌲 SIOBHAN HATHAWAY 🌲

Honeysuckle Cottage
(Caroline Lennon)

Dublin-born Siobhan met her husband **Tim** while working in Germany, and she now works from home as a freelance translator (she speaks French, German and Spanish. Oh, and English). Her main employer is a specialist magazine publisher with offices in **Felpersham** and Brussels. Attractive and elegant, Siobhan is one of those people who have a life plan, and she arrived in **Ambridge** from London planning to have children. The intrusion of messy, unplanned reality, in the form of a miscarriage, shook her for a while. But with the help of **Shula Hebden Lloyd** (who knows more about the roller coaster of infertility than Lord Winston), she adjusted her expectations and is happy for the babies to come when they are ready.

DR TIM HATHAWAY

Honeysuckle Cottage
(Jay Villiers)

Tim joined the army to finish his medical training, and served for six years in the UK and Germany, where he met his wife **Siobhan**. When he returned to civilian life, he worked as a GP in Islington before buying the practice in **Ambridge**. Misled by his army background, many villagers were expecting a rigid martinet, skilled in extracting bullets without anaesthetic. But while Tim is certainly well organised and practical, he is also a sympathetic counsellor, and has been a great help to **Ruth Archer** through her illness.

BUNTY AND REG HEBDEN

(Bunty born 20.2.22)

Reg and his wife Bunty were happy to see their son Mark follow his father into the solicitor's trade, and very happy with Mark's choice of wife – **Shula** (now **Hebden Lloyd**). But when Mark recruited an Asian woman – **Usha Gupta** – as his business partner, his parents' disapproval was just as clear. Bunty clashed with Shula's current husband **Alistair Lloyd** over **Daniel**'s education, and was disappointed when Shula opted for the local state primary. So when Alistair decided he wanted to adopt Daniel, it took a deal of cupcake diplomacy from **Jill** and **Phil Archer** before the Hebdens withdrew their objections and accepted the severing of their legal rights over their grandson. But Shula has made sure that their relationship with Daniel is just as close, despite the adoption.

HOME FARM

STOCK
600 ewes • 110 hinds, stags, calves

CROPS
956 acres cereals • 136 acres grassland
75 acres oil seed rape • 100 acres sugar beet
80 acres linseed • 75 acres peas
80 acres woodland • 58 acres set-aside, including:
40 acres industrial rape • 10 acres biomass (willow)

OTHER
25 acre riding course • Fishing Lake

LABOUR
Brian Aldridge (managing and relief)
Debbie Aldridge (deputy)
2 Tractor Drivers
Greg Turner (gamekeeper)
William Grundy (underkeeper)
Casual and Contract Labour
Occasional Students
Fly (sheepdog)

Home Farm is mainly arable and, with 1585 acres, the largest in **Ambridge**. When he bought the farm in the 1970s, **Brian Aldridge** took advantage of the grants available to rip out hedges, so that one field alone measures over 100 acres. More recently, he's taken advantage of the grants available to replace a few – but that's farming for you. Brian is also a member of the **Borchester Land** consortium which owns the **Berrow Estate**, and he farms it for the group.

♆ RT REVEREND CYRIL HOOD ♆

The Bishop of **Felpersham** is of the no-nonsense, sleeves-up school of Christianity, and is as comfortable chatting to **Joe Grundy** as to **Jack Woolley**. In fact it's a mark of the man that both those individuals claim a special relationship with him. Bishop Cyril married Jack and **Peggy**, and Joe – although notionally a Methodist – always seems to get a free feed when Cyril's in town. Even agnostic **Caroline Pemberton** was impressed with him, as he first clashed with Peggy over the ordination of women and then helped Caroline with her decision to marry **Ambridge**'s previous vicar, Robin Stokes. Cyril wasn't to know how ill-fated that decision was to be, and Robin's departure led to the appointment of **Janet Fisher**, which of course drove Peggy to another parish. Ah well...

CLIVE HORROBIN

Prison again, through no fault of his
own, you understand
(Born 9.11.72)
(Alex Jones)

What kind of fool would commit armed robbery in the **Village Shop**, just a stone's throw from his Mum's front door? Ladies and gentlemen, meet Clive Horrobin. Not content with frightening **Betty Tucker** out of her wits and **Jack Woolley**'s pacemaker into lifesaving activity, Clive later shamelessly exploited **Susan Carter**'s sisterly loyalty while on the run from the police. When Clive returned to **Ambridge** after a spell in clink, **Lynda Snell** hoped to rehabilitate him through the magic of drama, but ex-copper **George Barford** had Clive in the frame for a series of local burglaries. George received a serious beating for his suspicions, but Clive and his mates were eventually caught, and he is once more wearing Her Majesty's blue suit.

No 6, The Green, and elsewhere

Bert and Ivy Horrobin have a lot to answer for, namely **Clive**, Stewart, Gary, Keith and Tracy. Both Clive and Keith have spent time detained at Her Majesty's pleasure, and the only reason that Stewart and Gary have avoided porridge so far is that they are slightly less stupid than their brothers. The one exception to the Horrobin roll of dishonour used to be **Susan** (now **Carter**), but even she ended up in prison, even if it was really Clive's fault. Bert is a lengthman (it's something to do with road building) and Ivy cleans for **Usha Gupta** at Blossom Hill Cottage. Whenever Tracy quits a job, she leaves behind a grateful employer – grateful she's gone, that is. Most recently, it was the **Pargetters** breathing sighs of relief, although Owen misses Tracy giving him a hand in the kitchen.

JASON

(Brian Miller)

The squeal of brakes from a battered white van and a cheerful 'orroight, bab?' are a sign that Jason the builder has arrived for work – or more usually to tell the hapless householder that he's just got to pop off to Penny Hassett and he'll be back shortly. Ebullient Jason had three children with his ex-wife, but now lives with his girlfriend.

HAYLEY JORDAN

Nightingale Farm • Born 1977
(Lucy Davis)

Hayley is a qualified nursery nurse, nannying for **Josie** and other local mums, and helping at the local playgroup. Although she still can't tell a forage harvester from a four-furrow convertible, this bubbly Brummie has been warmly accepted by the villagers of **Ambridge** (all bar **Helen Archer**), and has become an all-purpose surrogate for several. Originally tempted from her concrete cradle by John Archer, Hayley still has a place in **Pat**'s affections, and she's like the granddaughter that her landlady **Marjorie Antrobus** never had. Hayley was incandescent when **Kate Aldridge** tripped off to Africa, leaving **Phoebe** in the care of her father **Roy Tucker**, but helping look after the child made Hayley realise that she felt more for Roy than just sympathy. So as well as being an item with Roy, Hayley is now a surrogate mother too and the three of them make a lovely family.

JOSIE

Waterley Cross

Josie works irregular hours as a photographer on the local paper the *Borchester Echo*. **Hayley Jordan** nannies for Josie's toddler Henry, and looks after his sister Becky when she's not at primary school.

SATYA KHANNA

Wolverhampton
(Jamilla Massey)

Usha Gupta's parents never really approved of Usha's move away from their adopted home in Wolverhampton (they were Ugandan Asians who fled to Britain in the 1970s). So it falls to Usha's Auntie Satya to act as go-between, and to turn up when she suspects that all is not well at Blossom Hill Cottage. Satya may be more open minded than Usha's mother and father, but she still has old-fashioned views on some things – like home cooking. At least when she's around Usha gets a decent meal. One of Satya's specialities are those incredibly sugar-rich sweets, which can rot tooth enamel from fifty paces. Satya always gets on well with **Marjorie Antrobus**, who has seen something of the world and has similar attitudes on many subjects – like the importance of a hot meal on the table.

Architect Lewis has a way with words, but more importantly for **Nigel** and **Elizabeth** he has a way with **Julia Pargetter**. Lewis is semi-retired, which means he can choose the projects which appeal to him, and which gives him time to squire Julia on pleasant outings or help her at **Lower Loxley**'s art gallery. He supervised the speedy conversion of Lower Loxley's shop and café from existing buildings, and was the ideal choice for the refurbishment of Arkwright Hall, **Jack Woolley**'s neglected Victorian pile, for the Landmark Trust. Lewis is one of those rare people who seem to get their own way while still being ineffably nice to everyone. It makes you sick, doesn't it?

ALISTAIR LLOYD 🌳

Glebe Cottage
(Michael Lumsden)

Alistair's a vet, based in the business units at Sawyer's Farm, so his arm is regularly to be found in the orifices of various animals in distress (well, you'd be distressed if a vet put his hand up... never mind) Alistair has a wry outlook on life, but he needed more than a sense of humour when he discovered friend and fellow cricketer Richard Locke had been sleeping with his girlfriend **Shula**. It was especially hard for Alistair, as his previous marriage had foundered when his wife started to 'play away'. Eventually Alistair's love for Shula and his affection for **Daniel** won out. Richard retired hurt and Alistair married Shula on Christmas Eve 1998. As wicket keeper (and captain), Alistair is fearless facing the bowling, but would rather duck the many personal questions he's had to endure in the process of adopting Daniel.

❧ DANIEL HEBDEN LLOYD ❧

Glebe Cottage • Born 14.11.94
(Dominic Davies)

Daniel is a miracle child, conceived by IVF after years of distressing childlessness for **Shula** and her first husband Mark. Tragically, Mark died without knowing that Shula was pregnant, or that this pregnancy would be successful. So when Daniel became very ill in 1998, it was a time of anguish for Shula, as she feared she might lose this precious legacy of her dead husband. The condition was eventually diagnosed as juvenile arthritis and, although treatment was successful, Daniel is still subject to occasional 'flares' of the illness. Daniel has always got on well with **Alistair** and soon adjusted to his presence in the house. Alistair knew he'd cracked it when Daniel started calling him 'dad', paving the way for Alistair's adoption of the boy.

🐓 SHULA HEBDEN LLOYD 🐓

(formerly Hebden, née Archer)
Glebe Cottage • Born 8.8.58
(Judy Bennett)

Phil and **Jill Archer**'s elder daughter and **Kenton**'s twin. Churchwarden Shula needed all her reserves of faith and fortitude when her husband Mark died in a car crash in 1994. But the greatest help was her discovery – sadly after Mark's death – that following years of disappointment and a previous failed IVF attempt she was pregnant with **Daniel**. After a messy love triangle that included the then local GP Richard Locke, Shula eventually married **Alistair**, but not before Richard had left the village and Shula had lost her friendship with Richard's partner **Usha Gupta**. A qualified chartered surveyor, Shula eventually returned to her first love of riding, going into partnership with her aunt **Christine Barford** at The Stables.

LAWRENCE LOVELL

A rather sad little bed-sit in Felpersham
(Stephen Hancock)

Lynda Snell thought she had the monopoly on the village amateur dramatic scene until Lawrence 'call me Larry' Lovell made his grand entrance. An ex-professional thespian and model for knitting patterns, Larry's greatest moment was understudying the Red Shadow in a West End production of *The Desert Song*. And despite Lynda's desperate decrying, Larry did actually 'go on' in the rôle, according to **Julia Pargetter**, whose stage career once crossed with his. Larry likes to see himself as a ladies' man, but his attempts to romance his leading ladies – notably **Jill Archer** – always seem, sadly, to come to naught. It's probably the cravat.

The grand house and estate of Lower Loxley must be worth a fortune, but say that to **Elizabeth Pargetter** and she's likely to hit you. Because it's only worth money if it's sold, and after three centuries of Pargetters, **Nigel** is not going to be the one to throw in the monogrammed towel. Faced with a dwindling conference market, in 2000 Nigel and Elizabeth built an impressive tree top walk and relaunched the place as 'a great day out for all the family'. As well as the old retainers **Titcombe** and **Mrs Pugsley**, the supporting cast includes conference manager Beverley, and resourceful Liam and Jane in the shop. The Orangery café is run by talented chef Owen, assisted by various part-timers including **Emma Carter**.

ADAM MACY

Somewhere in Africa • (Born 22.6.67)

What a scandal Adam's birth to the young, unmarried **Jennifer** Archer (now **Aldridge**) caused. Although she never publicly named the father, the child's shock of red hair implicated Paddy Redmond, **Phil Archer**'s cowman, who left the village soon afterwards. Jennifer's first husband Roger Travers-Macy adopted Adam, who grew into a sporty, good looking young man. After graduating in agricultural economics, Adam devoted himself to development work in Africa, and keeps in touch with the occasional card and email.

Ambridge's twin town since 1994, Meyruelle shimmers in the dusty haze of Languedoc-Rousillon in southern France. When a delegation visited Ambridge, **Brian Aldridge** was tempted to establish his own *entente cordiale* with the shapely Marie-Claire Beguet, while the then mayor Gustave Touvier found **Lynda Snell**'s *derrière* too tempting to leave unpinched. But for most villagers, the twinning has been an opportunity to widen their horizons and consider questions of *philosophie* raised by the relationship. For example; if the people of Meyruelle are the Meyruellois, what are the folk of Ambridge – Amburgers?

A farm in name only, this farmhouse with outbuildings and half an acre of gardens is home to **Marjorie Antrobus** and her now substantially reduced pack of dogs. The self-contained flat has been occupied by a variety of **Ambridge**'s young people before their first steps into home ownership, notably **Neil** and **Susan Carter**, **Ruth Archer** and most recently **Hayley Jordan** who was subsequently joined by **Roy Tucker** and daughter **Phoebe**.

❦ ELIZABETH PARGETTER ❦

(née Archer)

Lower Loxley Hall • Born 21.4.67

(Alison Dowling)

As **Phil** and **Jill Archer**'s youngest child, Elizabeth used to be a bit of a brat. And that was about the politest word her family used when she objected to Phil's plans to pass **Brookfield Farm** on to **David** (Elizabeth was to receive a mere token; half a £200,000 house). She protested that running **Lower Loxley** was like riding a unicycle while tearing up fifty pound notes, and anyway she was thinking only of **Lily and Freddie**. To be fair, Elizabeth hasn't had it easy in the past. She had an abortion after being dumped by swindler Cameron Fraser, and her congenital heart problem left her with the prospect of a valve replacement operation after the birth of the twins. But she can always count on the support of husband **Nigel** (who calls her 'Lizzie').

JULIA PARGETTER

Lower Loxley Hall • Born 17.8.24
(Mary Wimbush)

Grande dame Julia resents letting *hoi polloi* into her home, even though **Lower Loxley Hall** wouldn't survive without them. Although Julia was dreading **Nigel**'s wedding to a 'farmer's daughter' (**Elizabeth**), she wasn't to know just how embarrassing it was going to be, as her long-lost sister **Ellen Rogers** arrived to regale everyone with tales of Julia's true past as a greengrocer's daughter and dancer in wartime variety. Julia has fallen prey to addiction in the past; to alcohol and later to gambling, but she's done her best to be an asset since the arrival of a grandson and heir (oh, and yes, **Lily** too). Julia's best when there's a strong man on hand to curb her excesses, and now Nigel holds the ultimate weapon; he could reveal Julia's true age to **Lewis**.

ψ LILY AND FREDDIE ψ PARGETTER

Born 11.12.99

Elizabeth **Pargetter**'s heart condition would have made even a simple pregnancy daunting, but with twins the pressure was really on. Happily, both were born safely if early by caesarian section. Freddie (the second and smaller child) spent a worrying week in an incubator, but soon rallied. He is now the particular favourite of **Julia**, who obviously has no truck with that fashionable rubbish about treating children equally.

NIGEL PARGETTER

🐇   🐇

Lower Loxley Hall • Born 8.6.59
(Graham Seed)

Nigel used to be a bit of a Hooray, always ready with the champagne and a gorilla suit (don't ask), but after his father Gerald's death, he found himself saddled with copious death duties and the decaying family home to maintain. His solution was to throw **Lower Loxley Hall** open for conferences, corporate entertainment and as a public attraction. Nigel went out with **Shula** when they were younger, but his smartest move was to recruit her sister **Elizabeth**, first as his marketing manager and later his wife. Although occasionally his resolve wavers, he does his best to limit the excesses of his impossible mother **Julia**. He's firmly committed to keeping the Hall afloat, even if Elizabeth dreams wistfully of a little cottage somewhere, with Julia buried under the patio.

🐎 CAROLINE PEMBERTON 🐎

(née Bone)
The Dower House • Born 3.4.55
(Sara Coward)

A minor spur of the aristocracy (she is related to Lord Netherbourne) and **Shula**'s closest friend, Caroline is the manager of **Grey Gables** hotel. Her impeccable taste in clothes, horses and food is, sadly, not matched by her proficiency at choosing men. Her numerous ill-fated relationships included an affair with **Brian Aldridge**. Having almost resigned herself to a single life, she married an older man, Guy Pemberton, in 1995. But sadly Guy suffered a heart attack and died after only seven blissfully married months. He left her the Dower House, an annuity and a share in **The Bull**. Caroline agonised that she should have used some of her wealth to bale out the **Grundys** but in the end made a more noble contribution; offering godson **William** some rooms in her house.

JAMIE PERKS

Born 20.7.95
(Ben Ratley)

Jamie attends Loxley Barratt Primary and lives with his mother **Kathy**. Ironically, it was Jamie's arrival relatively late in **Sid**'s life which has now seen the child separated from his father. Wanting to keep up with a lively toddler, Sid started a fitness regime. Newly slim, he caught the eye of local siren (that's not a comment on her singing) **Jolene Rogers**. The rest is history.

KATHY PERKS

(née Holland)
Born 30.1.53
(Hedli Niklaus)

When Home Economics teacher Kathy married publican **Sid**, she found she'd married **The Bull** as well, and ambitious Kathy didn't enjoy the many compromises involved in serving a mass market. Kathy and Sid have never been perfectly matched. Sid didn't like it when frustrated Kathy took on some supply teaching, and she was discomfited by his homophobic hatred of a local gay publican. When (at the frightening age of 42) Kathy gave birth to **Jamie**, it seemed to bring the couple closer for a while. But, despite Kathy's earlier dalliance with local policeman Dave Barry, Sid's affair with **Jolene Rogers** was the thunderbolt that finally split the marriage after thirteen years. Kathy moved out, initially to lodge at **Bridge Farm**, determined to take Sid for every penny.

The Bull • Born 9.6.44

(Alan Devereux)

Sid is the co-owner (with **Caroline Pemberton**) and landlord of **The Bull**. Sid's first wife Polly died in a car crash, and their daughter **Lucy** (now **Gemmell**) never really accepted Sid's marriage to **Kathy**. In 1996, Sid abruptly gave up the captaincy of the cricket team after they mutinied over his resistance to selecting the gay Sean Myerson, but he returned in the new post of manager after Sean's departure. Sid woke up on New Year's Day 1999 with a resolution to improve his fitness. It seemed like a good idea at the time, but twelve months later he was in bed with **Jolene Rogers** and by the summer **Kathy** had discovered the affair. The result was separation from his beloved **Jamie**, and divorce proceedings which threatened even his future at the pub.

Grey Gables

Trudy flung off her reputation as the scatty receptionist at **Grey Gables**, proving herself a more than capable assistant manager to **Caroline Pemberton**. **Lynda Snell** has still not forgiven her.

MRS POTTER

Manorfield Close

A long-time resident of Ambridge's 'old people's homes', Mrs Potter will gamely take her walking frame to any treat the Over Sixties Club cares to lay on.

SOLLY AND HEATHER PRITCHARD

Prudoe, Northumberland
(Solly – James Thackwray
Heather – Joyce Gibbs)

Ruth Archer doesn't see her parents as much as she'd like. With the constant demands of the farm, it's difficult to find the time for the long drive north. And her dad Solly is a busy man, too, running a factory manufacturing toilet paper. But Heather was very quick to turn up at **Brookfield** when Ruth's cancer was diagnosed.

MRS PUGSLEY

Lower Loxley

Of the numerous staff at **Lower Loxley Hall**, housekeeper Mrs Pugsley is one of those whose name we hear regularly. But, like her colleague the redoubtable **Titcombe**, we only ever hear *of* her, never *from* her. Vivid imaginations will have the pair of them entwined in a passionate love affair, but that sort of thing is the province of tawdry romantic fiction, and has no place here.

MR PULLEN

Manorfield Close • (Born 13.7.15)

A silent resident of Manorfield Close, a development uncharitably known as 'God's waiting room'. When planning outings of the Ambridge Over Sixties Club, the key logistical factor is not the capacity of the coach's fuel tank, but the capacity of Mr Pullen's bladder.

Denia, Costa Blanca • Born 1926
(Rosemary Leach)

If you heard an infectious laugh drown out the hubbub at **Nigel** and **Elizabeth**'s wedding reception, chances are it came from Ellen (no relation to **Jolene**). **Julia Pargetter**'s sister is a woman who enjoys life, partly because, unlike Julia, she has nothing to hide. She's lived in Spain since her banker husband Harry decided to give up the rat race (well, that was his story) and buy a bar out there. Now she's a widow, the staff run the bar, leaving her time and money to spend as she likes. It's a shame Julia (or Joan, as Ellen insists on calling her) finds Ellen's revelations about their humble past so mortifying, because Ellen is genuinely proud of her sister's success.

FALLON ROGERS

The Bull • Born 19.6.85
(Joanna van Kamper)

Daughter of **Jolene Rogers** and her previous husband Wayne Tuscon (quite...). Fallon was the first to suss that Jolene was having an affair with **Sid Perks**, even though she found the prospect of her mother having sex too gross to contemplate. Once Fallon told **Ed Grundy**, who is in her year at Borchester Green School, it was only a matter of time before it became common knowledge. Rich revenge for being saddled with a naff name like Fallon, some would say.

♥ JOLENE ROGERS ♥

The Bull
(Buffy Davis)

A divorcee and mother of teenage **Fallon**, rhinestone-clad Jolene has scratched a meagre living on the British country and western circuit, although the recent stampede towards line dancing has proved a profitable sideline. **Clarrie Grundy** used to worry that the one-time 'Lily of Layton Cross' (real name Doreen) would steal her **Eddie** away, but to everyone's surprise it was **Sid Perks** whom Jolene corralled. Although first attracted by his newly trim physique, she eventually fell in love with him, and stole his cheatin' heart from **Kathy**. Whatever the rights and wrongs of how she got there, her easy personality and generous assets make Jolene a much more natural figure behind the bar than Kathy ever was.

GRAHAM RYDER

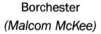

Borchester
(Malcom McKee)

A land agent working for the **Borchester** firm of Rodway and Watson, Graham was brought in as the hard man to replace **Shula Hebden Lloyd** at the **Berrow Estate** when the then owner Simon Pemberton thought she was being too soft on the tenants. Not that urbane, courteous Graham is a hard man per se, but he takes his professional duties very seriously, and he continues to give good service to the current owners, **Borchester Land**. For a while, he courted the lovely **Caroline Pemberton**, even returning to the saddle in an attempt to impress this doughty horsewoman, until to her relief he decided they were better suited as 'just friends'.

♩ ST STEPHEN'S CHURCH ♫

Established 1281

Visitors to this fine old church, whose history goes back to Saxon times, can hardly suspect the controversies which have surrounded St Stephen's: the installation of a lavatory; clandestine attempts to kill off the bats in the roof; a merger with three local parishes under the care of a *woman* vicar; to say nothing of the web of Machiavellian intrigue that is the flower rota. But for many in **Ambridge**, St Stephen's is an important fount of spiritual refreshment, as well as a centre of village social life. And for others – **Janet Fisher** (vicar), **Shula Hebden Lloyd** and **Bert Fry** (churchwardens), **Neil Carter** (bellringer), **Phil Archer** (organist) – it's a place to serve their God and their community.

SILENT CHARACTERS

One of the delights of **Ambridge** is that coterie of characters whom the listener knows well and can picture clearly, but who are never actually heard to speak. A large, but obviously rather quiet band, they include the efficient **Liam**, delectable **Mandy Beesborough**, the rather less delectable **Baggy** and **Snatch**, **Freda Fry**, many of the **Horrobins**, and the king of them all, the wonderful **John Higgs**.

LYNDA SNELL

Ambridge Hall • Born 29.5.47
(Carole Boyd)

When Lynda and **Robert** arrived from Sunningdale in 1986, Lynda threw herself vigorously into village life, wanting to be accepted and loved while simultaneously moulding **Ambridge** to her green ideals. Even when cycling to work on her old butcher's bike or ruling the reception desk at **Grey Gables**, her head is full of her latest enthusiasm – and it's a big head, so that's a lot of enthusiasm. As well as various attempts to save the world, over the years she has thrown herself into amateur theatricals, goat-keeping, low allergen gardening, parish magazine editing, aromatherapy and, most recently, Feng Shui. But far from bringing increased wealth and harmony to her marriage, this last proved to be a fad too far for the long-suffering Robert.

ROBERT SNELL

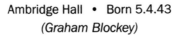

Ambridge Hall • Born 5.4.43
(Graham Blockey)

In contrast to his ubiquitous wife **Lynda**, computer boffin Robert leads a much more reserved life. He was particularly uncomfortable when he had to face angry creditors following the failure of his software business, but he eventually found a regular job in Birmingham. He has two children from a previous marriage, Coriander and Leonie (Cas and Len to their friends). Affable Robert enjoys rambling and as an MCC member brings a touch of class to the village cricket team. His easy going style has seen him through many of the irritations of living with Lynda, which we are unable to list owing to lack of space.

Lower Loxley Hall

The indispensable and bucolic Titcombe is head gardener at **Lower Loxley**. He is so busy with the extensive grounds – not to mention the extensive demands of **Julia Pargetter** – that he is never heard to speak.

BETTY TUCKER

Willow Farm • Born 4.8.50
(Pamela Craig)

Betty deserves sainthood for all she's had to put up with. Her job as manager of the **Village Shop** and post office provided the only regular source of income for the Tucker household during husband **Mike**'s difficult years, and he's not the easiest of men to live with even when he's not depressed. Betty was astonished to learn that her son **Roy** had become mixed up with the fascist gang persecuting **Usha Gupta**, but stood by him to see him eventually become a credit to the family. Energetic and kind hearted, Betty is a staunch WI member, and helps out occasionally behind the bar at **The Bull**. Once a cleaner at **Home Farm**, she and Mike were bemused to find themselves part of the extended **Aldridge** family, as fellow grandparents to **Phoebe**.

BRENDA TUCKER

Willow Farm • Born 21.1.81
(*Amy Schindler*)

Brenda emerged from the travails of her father **Mike**'s difficult period and her brother **Roy**'s involvement with fascists as a remarkably well-balanced teenager with an interest in amateur dramatics. After her A levels, she won a highly-prized job as a trainee journalist at BBC Radio Borsetshire. Mike doesn't know where either of his children get their brains from, but **Betty**'s got a shrewd idea.

MIKE TUCKER

Willow Farm • Born 1.12.49
(Terry Molloy)

Mike was made bankrupt after he and his wife **Betty** made a spirited attempt at running Ambridge Farm, and then struggled to make a living from his Borchester Dairies milk round and freelance forestry work. He suffered severe depression after an industrial injury in which he lost an eye, but he and Betty were able to use his compensation money to buy their house. Given the increasingly casual nature of farm employment, Mike will turn his hand to anything that pays – pigs, relief milking, fencing, tractor work... He has also run a small pick-your-own strawberry business with **Neil Carter**, whom he regularly rubs up the wrong way. Although he'd rather **Kate Aldridge** hadn't been involved, Mike rather enjoys being a granddad, and when Kate left he fought for **Roy**'s right to look after **Phoebe**.

ROY TUCKER

Nightingale Farm • Born 2.2.78
(Ian Pepperell)

In 1995 all **Ambridge** was shocked to discover that this bright spark was mixed up with the racists persecuting **Usha Gupta**, but he realised his mistake just in time and shopped the thugs to the police. Despite this disruption, he achieved good A level grades and in 2000 graduated in business studies and economics from Felpersham University. When **Kate Aldridge** denied he was the father of her daughter **Phoebe**, he astonished his mates by going to court to prove otherwise, but had to take on more parental responsibility than he expected when Kate left for Africa. With the help of girlfriend **Hayley Jordan**, he rose to the challenge of bringing up the toddler. Because he couldn't move in search of a job, he thought he'd have to resign himself to being **Grey Gables**' most over-qualified waiter until **Caroline Pemberton** spotted his potential and put him on the management ladder.

GREG TURNER

A tied cottage at Home Farm
(Marc Finn)

Taciturn Greg arrived to look after the expanded **Home Farm/Berrow Estate** shoot in 1998. He was determined to prove himself to **Brian Aldridge** and didn't mind if that meant rubbing people up the wrong way – especially competing gamekeeper **George Barford**. But he's done a good job, and earned the grudging respect of those who've come into contact with him. He doesn't talk about his past – in fact he doesn't talk about anything much – but it involved youth work, which has helped in his training of **William Grundy**.

UNDERWOODS

Borchester

A Traditional Department Store. Underwoods is the place for men's and ladies' Fashions, Kitchenware, Stationery, Hi-Fi, Perfumery and much, much more. Try the range of tempting treats in our extensive food hall, featuring the widest selection of Italian salamis in South Borsetshire. And if you've shopped till you've dropped, relax in our self-service restaurant with a Bath Bun, lite lunch or something more substantial. Why travel further afield?'

– Advertisement in *The Borchester Echo*.

Where to go for a local paper, a packet of beefburgers or a book of stamps? In **Ambridge** it must be the village shop and post office, presided over by **Betty Tucker** on behalf of the owner **Jack Woolley**. Like all village shops, it treads a precarious financial path, which causes part-time employee **Susan Carter** some disquiet. But while it stands, the shop provides that essential of village life – a little gossip with your groceries.

WILLOW FARM

'The farmhouse is home to **Mike** and **Betty Tucker**, and their daughter **Brenda**. Like **Nightingale Farm**, Willow Farm's land has long since been bought up by others – mainly neighbours **Phil Archer** and **Brian Aldridge** – but Mike uses the buildings to house his milk van and battery hens. **Neil Carter** owns eight acres, where he keeps his outdoor breeding herd of pigs, and has grown pick-your-own strawberries with Mike – when they're talking to each other, that is.

HAZEL WOOLLEY

Last seen in Soho
(Jan Cox)

Adopted daughter of **Jack Woolley** and his first wife, Valerie Trentham. The wayward Hazel seldom visits **Ambridge** and when she does she usually causes chaos. She claims to have some connections with the film business – but isn't specific exactly what kind of films. When stepmother **Peggy** tried to get in touch, Hazel was initially very interested – until she discovered that it was only to invite her to Jack's eightieth birthday party. You can be sure that when Jack finally snuffs it, Hazel will rush back to Ambridge with a little black suit and a lawyer in tow.

JACK WOOLLEY

The Lodge, Grey Gables • Born 19.7.19
(Arnold Peters)

A self-made man with considerable respect for his creator, Jack started small in the Birmingham suburb of Stirchley, but has been thinking big ever since. As well as **Grey Gables** Hotel and Country Club, he owns the **Village Shop** and the local paper the *Borchester Echo*. He has one adopted daughter, **Hazel**, from his first marriage. He recruited **Peggy** (then Archer) to be his assistant at **Grey Gables** after the death of her husband in 1972, and they were married in 1991. She has only recently managed to persuade him to retire properly from the day to day running of his various enterprises. Still active despite his age, Jack enjoys golf and shooting, which is handy as Grey Gables provides for both those pastimes (what a coincidence).

PEGGY WOOLLEY

(formerly Archer, née Perkins)
The Lodge, Grey Gables • Born 13.11.24
(June Spencer)

Just like her wealthy husband **Jack**, Peggy is proud to be of humble stock. She arrived in **Ambridge** from the East End of London, having married **Phil Archer**'s elder brother – spookily also called Jack – during the Second World War. In contrast to sturdy **Phil**, feckless Jack was a dreamer. Peggy took the brunt of his numerous get-rich-quick schemes, and she ran **The Bull** for many years until Jack's alcoholism proved fatal. A staunch churchgoer, Peggy couldn't countenance the arrival of a woman vicar in Ambridge, and moved her allegiance to All Saints, **Borchester**. Interestingly, Peggy's daughters **Jennifer Aldridge** and **Lilian Bellamy** also married wealthy men. In contrast, Peggy's son **Tony Archer** certainly didn't marry **Pat** for her money – or vice versa.

TO LEARN MORE ABOUT THE ARCHERS

Visit the **Archers Website** at

>   http://www.bbc.co.uk/radio4/archers/

for Archers episodes in Real Audio, daily plot synopses, news, information and chat about the programme.

Archers Addicts is the official Archers fan club, run by the cast. Members enjoy a quarterly newsletter, high quality merchandise, and the chance to meet Archers actors at events around the country.

Write to: Archers Addicts, PO Box 1951, Moseley,
    Birmingham B13 9DD.
Tel: 0121 683 1951/1952.

Website: http://www.archers-addicts.com

ARCHERS TITLES AVAILABLE ON AUDIO CASSETTE FROM THE BBC RADIO COLLECTION

The Archers 1951–1967: Family Ties
The Archers 1968–1986: Looking for Love
The Archers 1987–2000: Back to the Land
The Archers: The Third Generation
Vintage Archers: Volume One
Vintage Archers: Volume Two
Vintage Archers: Volume Three
Lynda Snell's Heritage of Ambridge

ARCHERS TITLES AVAILABLE FROM BBC BOOKS

The Archers 1951–1967: Family Ties by Joanna Toye
The Archers 1968–1986: Looking for Love by Joanna Toye
The Archers 1987–2000: Back to the Land by Joanna Toye
The Archers Annual 2001 by Kate Willmott and
Hedli Niklaus

THE AUTHOR

After dabbling in jobs as varied as banking, advertising, media training, PR and the Royal Air Force, **Keri Davies** conned his way into Ambridge seven years ago. He rose to be senior producer by bribery, blackmail and threatening to play the accordian. So far no-one has unmasked him for the fraudster he is. But he lives in fear.